P9-CAT-866

The Great Cupcake Book

50 Recipes

Exquisite Cupcake Recipes for Year 'Round Baking

from the creators of the Original Bundt® Pan

NORDIC WARE®

The Great Cupcake Book: Copyright © 2011 by
Northland Aluminum Products, Inc.
and CulinartMedia, Inc.

Published by
Northland Aluminum Products, Inc.
NORDIC WARE and BUNDT BAKEWARE
5005 Hwy 7
Minneapolis, MN 55416

Produced by
CulinartMedia, Inc
169 Port Road, Suite 41
Kennebunk, Maine 04043

All rights reserved, including the right of reproduction
in any manner whatsoever.

Editor: Reed Winter and Shannon Mahoney
Design: Harrah Lord and Katie Tobin
Layout: Patty Holden
Recipe Testing: Julie Stanton

ISBN 978-0-9744605-2-9

Printed in the USA by RR Donnelley

From Our Kitchen to Yours...

NORDIC WARE products have become a central icon in many American kitchens. In fact, every 4.5 seconds a Nordic Ware product is purchased somewhere in the world. Nearly 60 million Bundt® pans are in use, and the number continues to grow with an extensive new line of Bundt® shapes added in recent years.

Founded by H. David and Dorothy Dalquist in 1946, Nordic Ware remains family-owned and dedicated to providing outstanding customer service and support for their great innovative kitchenware products. Nordic Ware's commitment to inventing and re-inventing its line of American-made cookware, bakeware, microwave and barbeque products is paralleled only by the company's commitment to the community, its customers and employees and maintaining its "family" atmosphere. The company recognizes customer satisfaction with its quality products is the basis for continued success, and as a result, Nordic Ware enjoys enormous customer loyalty. The company has stood the test of time from its inception in 1946, to its recent transition from middle class marvel to gourmet comfort food status.

Although the company's first products were ethnic bakeware products such as the Rosette Iron, Ebleskiver Pan and Krumkake Iron, Nordic Ware is best known for its Bundt® Pan. It was after a large baking competition in 1966 where the winning recipe, the Tunnel of Fudge cake, was baked in a Bundt Pan, that the popularity of the Bundt Pan among the general public skyrocketed.

With **THE GREAT CUPCAKE BOOK**, Nordic Ware proudly delivers a selection of recipes that vary from tried-and-true classics to wild flavor combinations that will surprise your guests and liven up any dessert offering. Who can't recall the anticipation of warm cupcakes fresh from the oven, carefully peeling back a cupcake paper, or taking that first big bite of a luscious frosting-topped delight? The versatility of cupcakes makes them appeal to both young and old. Many of the recipes in *The Great Cupcake Book* are kid-friendly suited for children's assistance during baking. All of the recipes in this book can be made with a few simple items found in every kitchen, and ingredients from your local grocer. Happy baking!

Contents

Chocolate

Chocolate Cupcakes with Peanut Butter Frosting

PREP TIME: 20 min
BAKING TIME: 20–25 min

makes 14 cupcakes

INGREDIENTS

¾ cup (175 ml) unsalted butter, at room temperature (1½ sticks)

⅔ cup (150 ml) granulated sugar

⅔ cup (150 ml) light brown sugar, packed

2 teaspoons pure vanilla extract

2 fresh extra-large eggs, room temperature

1 cup (250 ml) buttermilk, room temperature

½ cup (125 ml) sour cream, room temperature

2 tablespoons brewed coffee

1¾ cups (400 ml) unbleached all-purpose flour

1 cup (250 ml) good quality cocoa powder

½ teaspoon kosher salt

1½ teaspoons baking soda

FOR PEANUT BUTTER FROSTING:

1 cup (250 ml) confectioners' sugar

1 cup (250 ml) creamy peanut butter

5 tablespoons unsalted butter, at room temperature

1 teaspoon pure vanilla extract

1 pinch kosher salt

⅓ cup (75 ml) heavy cream

METHOD

1. Position oven rack in the middle. Preheat oven to 350°F (177°C). Line muffin tins with paper or foil liners.

2. Using an electric mixer set on high speed, cream together the butter and sugars, until light and fluffy, about 5 minutes. Lower the speed to medium, add the vanilla and the eggs one at a time and mix well.

3. In a separate bowl, whisk together the buttermilk, sour cream and coffee. Using a new bowl, sift together the flour, cocoa powder, salt and baking soda. With the mixer on low speed, starting with the buttermilk mixture and ending with the flour mixture, add alternately in thirds to the butter and sugar mixture. Mix until just blended, scraping the sides with a rubber spatula to completely incorporate.

4. Divide batter evenly between lined cups, filling each cup three-quarters full. Bake for 20 to 25 minutes or until a cake tester inserted in the middle comes out clean. Rotate tins halfway through the baking process to promote even baking. Cool for 10 minutes in pan. Remove cupcakes from pan and transfer onto wire racks to cool completely before frosting.

For Peanut Butter Frosting:

1. In a large bowl, using an electric mixer set on medium-high speed, combine confectioners' sugar, peanut butter, butter, vanilla and salt. Mix until creamy, scraping down the sides of the bowl with a rubber spatula. Add the cream and beat on high speed until smooth and light.

2. Using a small offset spatula, spread frosting over the top of each cupcake. Serve.

Brownie Ice Cream Cone Cupcakes

PREP TIME: 20 min
BAKING TIME: 25–28 min

makes 12 cupcakes

INGREDIENTS

12 flat-bottomed ice cream cones

½ cup (125 ml) unsalted butter, cut into pieces (1 stick)

3 ounces (90 g) unsweetened chocolate, finely chopped

¾ cup (175 ml) all-purpose flour

½ teaspoon baking powder

1 pinch kosher salt

2 fresh large eggs

1¼ cups (300 ml) granulated sugar

1 teaspoon vanilla extract

⅔ cup (150 ml) semisweet chocolate chips

FOR BUTTERCREAM FROSTING:

4 tablespoons butter, room temperature

2½ cups (600 ml) confectioners' sugar

1 teaspoon pure vanilla extract

2 to 3 tablespoons milk

Multi-colored sprinkles

METHOD

1. Position oven rack in the middle of the oven. Preheat oven to 325°F (163°C). Cut twelve 6-inch (16 cm) squares of aluminum foil and press the into standard muffin tins, letting the foil overlap the edges of the muffin tins. Place a cone in each tin, wrapping the foil around the cone to hold it in place.

2. Place the butter and unsweetened chocolate in the top of a double boiler and place it over a saucepan of barely simmering water. Stir until the butter and chocolate are melted. Remove from the water; set aside to cool slightly.

3. In a small bowl, whisk the flour, baking powder and salt together; set aside. In a separate bowl, using an electric mixer set on medium speed, beat the eggs and sugar for about 1 minute or until thickened and pale. Scrape the sides of the bowl as necessary. Add the vanilla. On low speed, add the chocolate mixture. Mix in the flour mixture until fully incorporated. The batter should be smooth. Gently fold in the chocolate chips.

4. Using a small spoon, fill each ice cream cone with batter to the top of the cone. Carefully put the cupcakes in the oven, making sure that the cones are standing upright. Bake for about 25 to 28 minutes, or just until a cake tester inserted in the center comes out with a few moist crumbs. Transfer tins to a wire rack and cool in the pan for 20 to 30 minutes.

For Buttercream Frosting:

1. In a small mixing bowl, cream butter and sugar together. Add vanilla and gradually add milk, beat until light and smooth, adding more milk as needed until the desired consistency is reached.

2. Spoon the frosting into a pastry bag. Pipe frosting over the top of the cooled cupcake, to resemble soft serve ice cream. Garnish with sprinkles. Serve.

Mocha Cupcakes

PREP TIME: 25 min
BAKING TIME: 18–22 min

makes 24 cupcakes

INGREDIENTS

2¼ cups (500 ml) cake flour

2 tablespoons unsweetened Dutch-process cocoa powder

½ cup (125 ml) unsalted butter, softened (1 stick)

1½ cups (350 ml) light-brown sugar, packed

2 fresh large eggs, room temperature

1 teaspoon pure vanilla extract

1 pinch kosher salt

1½ teaspoons baking soda

½ cup (125 ml) sour cream, room temperature

¾ cup (175 ml) freshly brewed espresso

2 tablespoons instant espresso powder

FOR SEVEN-MINUTE FROSTING:

2 cups (500 ml) granulated sugar

3 large egg whites

3 tablespoons light corn syrup

3 tablespoons cold water

1 teaspoon pure vanilla extract

METHOD

1. Preheat oven to 325°F (163°C). Line muffins tins with paper or foil liners.

2. In a mixing bowl, whisk together cake flour and cocoa. With an electric mixer set on medium-high speed, cream butter until light and smooth. Add the brown sugar and eggs, beat until light and fluffy. Scrape down the sides of the bowl as necessary. Add the vanilla, baking soda, and salt; beat until thoroughly incorporated.

3. Reduce mixer speed to low; add flour mixture in thirds, alternating with sour cream, beating until just combined. Mix brewed espresso and espresso powder together; add to batter, beating until combined.

4. Divide batter between lined muffin tins, filling each cup three-quarters full. Bake until cake tester inserted in centers comes out clean, about 18 to 22 minutes. Rotate tins halfway through the baking process, to promote even baking. Remove from oven, transfer tins to wire racks and cool completely.

For Seven-Minute Frosting:

1. Using the top of a double boiler combine sugar, egg whites, corn syrup, water and vanilla. Place over boiling water and beat with an electric mixer on high speed until peaks form, or for 7 minutes. Remove from heat.

2. Using a small spoon or offset spatula, generously frost each cupcake making decorative peaks. Serve.

Chocolate Walnut Cupcakes

PREP TIME: 20 min
BAKING TIME: 20-25 min

makes 24 cupcakes

INGREDIENTS

6 fresh large eggs, separated

¼ cup (60 ml) granulated sugar, plus
3 tablespoons

1¾ cups (400 ml) finely ground walnuts

3 ounces (90 g) bittersweet chocolate,
finely chopped

1 tablespoon orange zest, finely grated

¼ teaspoon kosher salt

Confectioners' sugar, for dusting

METHOD

1. Preheat oven to 300°F (149°C). Line muffin tins with paper or foil liners. In a medium bowl, using an electric mixer set on medium-high speed, whisk egg yolks, and ¼ cup (60 ml) granulated sugar together. In a separate bowl, toss walnuts, chocolate, orange zest and salt together. Sprinkle on top of egg yolk mixture, do not mix.

2. Place egg whites in a ovenproof bowl set over a pan of simmering water; whisk egg whites until warm to the touch. Remove from heat source. Using the electric mixer set on high speed, whisk egg whites until soft peaks form. Add remaining 3 tablespoons of granulated sugar and whisk until peaks are stiff and glossy. Gently fold egg whites into egg yolk mixture.

3. Divide batter between lined muffin tins, filling them three-quarters full. Bake until cupcakes' tops spring back or cake tester inserted in centers comes out clean, about 20 to 25 minutes. Rotate tins halfway through the baking process to promote even baking. Remove from oven, transfer tins to wire racks and cool for 15 minutes. Remove cupcakes and cool completely on wire racks. Dust with confectioners' sugar before serving.

Peppermint-Filled Brownie Cupcakes

PREP TIME: 20 min

BAKING TIME: 35 min

makes 12 cupcakes

INGREDIENTS

8 ounces (240 g) semisweet chocolate, coarsely chopped

1/2 cup (125 ml) unsalted butter, softened (1 stick)

1 cup (250 ml) sugar

3/4 teaspoon salt

3 fresh large eggs

1/2 cup (125 ml unbleached all-purpose flour

1/4 cup (60 ml) unsweetened Dutch-process cocoa powder, sifted

12 small chocolate covered peppermint patties (mini York Peppermint Patties)

METHOD

1. Preheat oven to 350°F (177°C). Line muffin tins with paper or foil liners. Place chocolate and butter in a heatproof bowl set over a pan of simmering water. Stir frequently until just melted, about 4 to 5 minutes.

2. Remove bowl from heat. Whisk in sugar and salt until mixture is smooth and creamy. Whisk in eggs to combine. Whisk in flour and cocoa just until smooth.

3. Spoon 1 generous tablespoon of batter into each prepared muffin cup. Place 1 peppermint patty on top, gently pressing it into the batter. Top with 2 tablespoons batter, covering peppermint patty. Bake, rotating tins halfway through the baking process, for about 35 minutes or until a cake tester inserted halfway in centers comes out with only a few crumbs attached. Transfer tin to a wire rack to completely cool before removing cupcakes.

Molten Flourless Chocolate Cupcakes

PREP TIME: 20 min
BAKING TIME: 40–45 min

makes 20 cupcakes

INGREDIENTS

8 ounces (240 g) good-quality bittersweet chocolate, divided

½ cup (125 ml) unsalted butter (1 stick)

1 cup (250 ml) heavy cream

4 large eggs, room temperature

1⅓ cups (300 ml) granulated sugar

½ cup (125 ml) mayonnaise

½ cup (125 ml) cornstarch

½ teaspoon ground cinnamon

½ teaspoon kosher salt

Confectioners' sugar, for dusting

METHOD

1. Preheat oven to 350°F (177°C). Line muffin tins with paper or foil liners.

2. Shave 5 ounces (150 g) of chocolate and place in a bowl. Cut the remaining chocolate into (12) ½-inch pieces (1½ cm), set aside.

3. In a small saucepan over medium-high heat, combine the butter and heavy cream. Once the cream mixture comes to a simmer, pour it over the shaved chocolate and gently stir to melt the chocolate.

4. In a medium bowl, whisk the eggs, sugar, mayonnaise, cornstarch, cinnamon and salt together just until the sugar has dissolved. Pour the melted chocolate mixture into the egg mixture, stirring until just combined. Divide batter evenly between lined muffin tins, filling each with ¼ cup (60 ml) of the batter. Bake until cake tester inserted in centers comes out clean, about 40 to 45 minutes. Do not over bake. Remove from oven, and immediately while hot, gently push a piece of the remaining chocolate into the center of each cupcake center. Cool in the pan on a wire rack for 10 to 15 minutes. Remove from pan and dust with confectioners' sugar. Serve warm.

Chocolate Chip Cupcakes with Buttercream Frosting

PREP TIME: 25 min
BAKING TIME: 22 min

makes 30 cupcakes

INGREDIENTS

3¼ cups (750 ml) cake flour, sifted

1½ tablespoons baking powder

1 pinch kosher salt

1 tablespoon pure vanilla extract

1 cup (250 ml) plus 2 tablespoons milk

7 ounces (200 g) unsalted butter, softened (1¾ sticks)

1¾ cups (400 ml) granulated sugar

5 fresh large whites, room temperature

2 cups (500 ml) semisweet chocolate chips

FOR BUTTERCREAM FROSTING:

12 ounces (350 g) unsalted butter, softened (3 sticks)

3¾ cups (900 ml) confectioners' sugar, sifted

1 teaspoon pure vanilla extract

2 cups (500 ml) semisweet chocolate chips

METHOD

1. Preheat oven to 350°F (177°C). Line muffin tins with paper or foil liners. Whisk together cake flour, baking powder and salt. Stir the vanilla into the milk.

2. Using an electric mixer set on medium-high speed, cream butter until smooth. Add sugar in a steady stream; beat until light and fluffy. Reduce mixer speed to low. Add flour mixture in three batches, alternating with vanilla milk, beating until just combined.

3. In a separate bowl, with the electric mixer on medium speed, whisk the egg whites until stiff peaks form. Gently fold the egg whites into the batter until just combined. Lightly dust chocolate chips in flour and fold into the batter.

4. Divide batter between lined muffin tins, filling them three-quarters full. Bake until cake tester inserted in centers comes out clean, about 22 minutes. Rotate tins halfway through the baking process to promote even baking. Transfer tins to wire racks and cool completely before removing cupcakes.

For Buttercream Frosting:

1. In a medium bowl, using and electric mixer on medium-high speed, beat butter for about 2 minutes, or until light and creamy.

2. Reduce mixer speed to medium. Add confectioners' sugar, ½ cup (125 ml) at a time, beating after each addition. Add vanilla and beat until buttercream is smooth. Gently fold in chocolate chips.

3. Spread frosting on cupcakes using a small offset spatula. Serve.

German Chocolate Cupcakes

PREP TIME: 30 min
BAKING TIME: 18–20 min

makes 24 cupcakes

INGREDIENTS

2 cups (500 ml) cake flour, sifted

1 teaspoon baking soda

3/4 teaspoon kosher salt

3/4 cup (175 ml) unsalted butter, room temperature (1½ sticks)

1⅓ cups (300 ml) granulated sugar

3 fresh large eggs, room temperature

1½ teaspoons pure vanilla extract

1 cup (250 ml) buttermilk

5 ounces (150 g) semisweet chocolate, melted and cooled

FOR COCONUT-PECAN FROSTING:

3 large egg yolks

1 can (12 ounces/360 g) evaporated milk

1¼ cups (300 ml) packed light-brown sugar

3/4 cup unsalted butter, softened and cut into small pieces (1½ sticks)

1 teaspoon pure vanilla extract

1 pinch kosher salt

7 ounces (210 g) sweetened flaked coconut

1½ cups (350 ml) pecans, toasted and coarsely chopped

METHOD

1. Preheat oven to 350°F (177°C). Spray muffin tins with nonstick cooking spray. In a medium bowl, whisk flour, baking soda and salt together.

2. In a large bowl, using an elctric mixer on medium-high speed, cream butter and sugar until light and fluffy. Add eggs, one at a time, beating until each one is combined. Scrape down the sides of the bowl as necessary. Beat in vanilla. Reduce speed to low. Add flour mixture in three batches, alternating with the buttermilk, and beating until just combined. Beat in melted chocolate until combined.

3. Divide batter evenly between prepared muffin tins, filling each one three-quarters full. Bake for about 20 minutes or until cake tester inserted in the middle comes out clean. Rotate tins halfway through the baking process to promote even baking. Cool for 10 minutes in the pan on a wire rack. Run a small offset spatula around the edges of the cupcakes, and turn out onto wire racks. Let cool completely.

For Coconut-Pecan Frosting:

1. Heat egg yolks, evaporated milk, brown sugar and butter in a saucepan over medium heat, stirring continuously, until thick, about 10 minutes. Using a fine sieve, strain mixture into a bowl.

2. Stir vanilla, salt, coconut and pecans into egg mixture. Cool completely, stirring occasionally.

Assembly:

Use a serrated knife and gently cut cupcakes in half horizontally. Spread a generous tablespoon of frosting on top of each bottom half; replace top half and frost the top of each cupcake. Serve immediately.

Fruit

Key Lime Cupcakes with Cream Cheese Frosting

PREP TIME: 30 min
BAKING TIME: 20-25 min

makes 42 cupcakes

INGREDIENTS

1½ cups (350 ml) self-rising flour

2 cups (500 ml) unbleached all-purpose flour

1 cup (250 ml) unsalted butter, room temperature (2 sticks)

2½ cups (600 ml) granulated sugar

4 fresh large eggs

5 tablespoons fresh lime juice

1 tablespoon lime peel, finely grated

1½ cups (350 ml) buttermilk

FOR CREAM CHEESE FROSTING:

16 ounces (480 g) cream cheese, room temperature

3 cups (750 ml) powdered sugar

1 cup (250 ml) unsalted butter, room temperature (2 sticks)

1 teaspoon pure vanilla extract

2 drops green food coloring

Decorative edible candy confetti, for garnish

METHOD

1. Preheat oven to 350°F (177°C). Line muffin tins with paper or foil liners.

2. In a medium bowl, whisk both flours together. In a separate large bowl, using an electric mixer on medium-high speed, beat butter until smooth. Add sugar, beating until light and fluffy. Beat in 1 egg at a time; add lime juice and lime peel. Beat in flour and buttermilk in three batches, alternating between the two.

3. Divide batter evenly between lined tins, filling each cup one-half full. Bake for 20 to 25 minutes or until a cake tester inserted in the middle comes out clean. Rotate tins halfway through the baking process to promote even baking. Cool for 10 minutes in pan. Remove cupcakes from pan and transfer onto wire racks to cool completely before frosting.

For Cream Cheese Frosting:

1. Beat first 5 ingredients in a medium bowl until smooth and creamy.

2. Using a small offset spatula, spread frosting over the top of each cupcake. Decorate with candy confetti. Serve.

Banana Cupcakes with Peanut Butter Frosting

PREP TIME: 20 min
BAKING TIME: 20 min

makes 12 cupcakes

INGREDIENTS

1¼ cups (300 ml) unbleached all-purpose flour

1½ teaspoons baking powder

½ teaspoon baking soda

¼ teaspoon salt

2 very ripe large bananas, peeled

½ cup (125 ml) sour cream

1½ teaspoons pure vanilla extract

¾ cup (175 ml) granulated sugar

½ cup (125 ml) unsalted butter, room temperature (1 stick)

1 large egg

1 large egg yolk

For Frosting:

1½ cups (350 ml) powdered sugar

8 ounces cream cheese, room temperature

½ cup (125 ml) unsalted butter, room temperature (1 stick)

½ cup (125 ml) smooth peanut butter, (do not use old-fashioned or freshly ground)

Lightly salted roasted peanuts, chopped (optional)

METHOD

1. Position oven rack in center of oven and preheat to 350°F (177°C). Line muffin tins with paper liners.

2. Whisk flour, baking powder, baking soda and salt in a medium bowl to blend. Mash bananas with fork in another medium bowl until smooth. Mix sour cream and vanilla into bananas.

3. Using an electric mixer, beat sugar and butter in a large bowl until light and fluffy, about 3 minutes. Add egg and egg yolk and beat until well blended. Add flour mixture in 3 additions alternately with banana-sour cream mixture in 2 additions, beginning and ending with flour mixture and beating just until blended after each addition. Divide batter evenly among prepared muffin tins.

4. Bake cupcakes until cake tester inserted into center of each comes out clean, about 20 minutes. Transfer cupcakes to wire rack and let cool completely.

For Frosting:

Sift powdered sugar into large bowl. Add softened cream cheese, butter and peanut butter. Using electric mixer, beat mixture until smooth. Spread frosting over tops of cooled cupcakes, dividing equally. Sprinkle lightly with chopped peanuts, if desired.

■ TIP

Can be made 1 day ahead. Store in an airtight container at room temperature.

Lemon Cupcakes with Lemon Buttercream Frosting

PREP TIME: 20 min
BAKING TIME: 25–30 min

makes 30 cupcakes

INGREDIENTS

1 cup (250 ml) butter, room temperature (2 sticks)

2 cups (500 ml) granulated sugar

3 fresh eggs

2 teaspoons lemon peel, grated

1 teaspoon pure vanilla extract

3½ cups (800 ml) unbleached all-purpose flour

1 teaspoon baking soda

½ teaspoon baking powder

½ teaspoon kosher salt

2 cups (500 ml) sour cream

For Lemon Buttercream Frosting:

3 tablespoons butter, room temperature

2½ cups (600 ml) confectioners' sugar

2 tablespoons lemon juice

1 teaspoon pure vanilla extract

¼ teaspoon lemon peel, grated

1½ tablespoons milk

¼ cup (60 ml) yellow sugar crystals

METHOD

1. Preheat oven to 350°F (177°C). Line muffin tins with paper liners.

2. In a large mixing bowl, cream butter and sugar together. Beat in eggs, one at a time; add lemon peel and vanilla, mixing well. Combine flour, baking soda, baking powder and salt. Add to cream mixture, alternating with dry ingredients and sour cream. Mix well, scraping the sides of the bowl as necessary.

3. Divide batter between lined muffin tins, filling them three-quarters full. Bake until cake tester inserted in centers comes out clean, about 25 to 30 minutes. Rotate tins halfway through the baking process to promote even baking. Remove from oven and cool for 10 minutes. Transfer cupcakes to wire racks and cool completely.

For Frosting:

1. In a small mixing bowl, cream butter and sugar together. Add lemon juice, vanilla, lemon peel and milk, beat until light and smooth.

2. Using a small offset spatula, generously frost each cupcake. Sprinkle with sugar crystals. Serve.

Strawberry Cupcakes

PREP TIME: 30 min

BAKING TIME: 25–30 min

makes 30 cupcakes

INGREDIENTS

2¾ cups (650 ml) unbleached all-purpose flour

½ cup (125 ml) cake flour

1 tablespoon baking powder

1 teaspoon salt

1 cup (250 ml) unsalted butter, room temperature (2 sticks)

2¼ cups (500 ml) granulated sugar

1½ teaspoons pure vanilla extract

1 egg white

3 fresh large eggs

1 cup (250 ml) milk

2 cups (500 ml) fresh strawberries, rinsed, hulled and finely chopped, plus extra for garnish

FOR FROSTING:

12 tablespoons unsalted butter, room temperature (1½ sticks)

4 cups (1 L) confectioners' sugar, sifted

1 teaspoon pure vanilla extract

½ teaspoon salt

4 tablespoons milk or heavy cream

Strawberry jam, to taste

METHOD

1. Preheat oven to 350°F (177°C). Line muffin tins with paper or foil liners. In a medium bowl sift flours, baking powder and salt together.

2. Using an electric mixer set on medium-high speed, cream butter, sugar and vanilla together until light and fluffy. Add egg white and eggs, one at a time, beating until each is fully incorporated. Scrape the sides of the bowl as necessary. Reduce speed to low and add flour mixture, in two batches, alternating with the milk. Beat until thoroughly mixed. Fold in finely chopped strawberries by hand.

3. Divide batter evenly between lined cups, filling each cup three-quarters full. Bake for 25 to 30 minutes or until a cake tester inserted in the middle comes out clean. Rotate tins halfway through the baking process to promote even baking. Cool for 15 minutes in pan. Remove cupcakes from pan and transfer onto wire racks to cool completely before frosting.

For Frosting:

1. In a medium bowl, using an electric mixer on medium speed, beat the butter until smooth and creamy. Add the confectioners' sugar, vanilla extract and salt. Beat on low speed until just combined. Increase mixer speed and beat until smooth. Add the milk or cream and beat until light and fluffy, about 3 or 4 minutes. Fold in a spoonful or two of strawberry jam.

2. Spoon frosting into a pastry bag fitted with a large, open-star tip. Pipe frosting onto each cupcake. Just prior to serving, arrange on a serving tray and garnish with fresh strawberries.

Blueberry Crisp Cupcakes

PREP TIME: 20 min
BAKING TIME: 28–30 min

makes 30 cupcakes

INGREDIENTS

2 cups (500 ml) unbleached all-purpose flour

2 teaspoons baking powder

¼ teaspoon salt

1¾ cups (400 ml) granulated sugar

½ cup (125 ml) butter, room temperature (1 stick)

¾ cup (175 ml) milk

1½ teaspoons pure vanilla extract

3 egg whites

3 cups (750 ml) blueberries (fresh or frozen)

FOR STREUSEL:

⅓ cup (75 ml) unbleached all-purpose flour

¼ cup (60 ml) uncooked oats (quick or old fashioned)

¼ cup (60 m) light brown sugar, packed

½ teaspoon ground cinnamon

¼ cup (60 ml) butter (½ stick)

½ cup (125 ml) walnuts, chopped

METHOD

1. Preheat oven to 350°F (177°C). Line muffin tins with paper or foil liners.

2. In a medium bowl, combine flour, baking powder and salt and mix well. In a separate bowl, using an electric mixer set on medium speed, beat sugar and butter together for 1 minute. Add milk and vanilla and beat for an additional 30 seconds. Add flour mixture gradually, beat at medium speed for 2 minutes. Add egg whites and beat for 1 minute longer, scraping the sides of the bowl as needed.

3. Divide batter between lined muffin tins, filling each one-half full. Sprinkle blueberries over the batter. Bake for 10 minutes.

For Streusel:

1. Combine flour, oats, sugar and cinnamon together in a small bowl. Mix well. Cut in butter with two knives until mixture resembles crumbs. Stir in walnuts.

2. Once cupcakes have baked for 10 minutes, sprinkle streusel over partially cooked cupcakes. Return to oven; continue to bake for 18 to 20 minutes or until cake tester inserted in centers comes out clean. Remove from oven and cool in pan on wire racks for 10 minutes. Remove and cool completely before serving.

Lemon Meringue Cupcakes

PREP TIME: 20 min
BAKING TIME: 18–20 min

makes 12 cupcakes

INGREDIENTS

½ cup (125 ml) unsalted butter, softened (1 stick)

½ cup (125 ml) granulated sugar

2 fresh eggs

1 cup (250 ml) self-rising flour

1 lemon, zest only

FOR MERINGUE:

2 fresh egg whites

½ cup (125 ml) granulated sugar

1 teaspoon fresh lemon juice

1 fresh lemon, for garnish

METHOD

1. Preheat oven to 350°F (177°C). Line muffin tins with paper or foil liners.

2. In a large bowl, using an electric mixer set on medium speed, cream butter and sugar together until light and fluffy. Add the eggs, one at a time, and beat until fully incorporated. Fold in the flour and lemon zest until well combined.

3. Divide batter evenly between lined cups, filling each one three-quarters full. Bake for 18 to 20 minutes or until they are golden-brown on top and springy to the touch. Rotate tins halfway through the baking process to promote even baking. Remove from oven and cool for 10 minutes. Transfer cupcakes to wire racks and cool completely.

For Meringue:

1. Whisk the egg whites until soft peaks form. Gradually add the sugar, whisking continuously until the peaks are stiff, thick and glossy.

2. Set the broiler to the highest setting. Spoon meringue over the cupcakes and form spikes using a knife.

3. Place the cupcakes under the broiler for 1 minute or so, or until the meringue is tinged golden-brown (watch closely).

4. Garnish with lemon zest curls, if desired.

Orange Chiffon Cupcakes with Buttercream Frosting

PREP TIME: 30 min
BAKING TIME: 18 min

makes 24 cupcakes

INGREDIENTS

2 fresh large eggs (separated)

½ cup (125 ml) sugar

2 cups (500 ml) cake flour, sifted

1 cup (250 ml) granulated sugar

2 teaspoons baking powder

1 pinch kosher salt

2 teaspoons pure vanilla extract

1 tablespoon orange liqueur (such as Grand Marnier)

1 cup (250 ml) half-and-half

½ cup (125 ml) canola oil

2 fresh egg yolks

2 teaspoons orange zest, finely grated

FOR BUTTERCREAM FROSTING:

3 tablespoons butter, room temperature

2½ cups (600 ml) confectioners' sugar

2 tablespoons orange juice

1 teaspoon pure vanilla extract

¼ teaspoon orange zest, finely grated

1½ tablespoons milk

METHOD

1. Preheat oven to 350°F (177°C). Line muffin tins with paper or foil liners.

2. In a medium bowl, using an electric mixer beat egg whites to the soft peak stage. Gradually add sugar and beat into stiff peaks. Set aside.

3. In a large bowl, sift together cake flour, sugar, baking powder and salt. Add remaining ingredients and beat until well combined. Gently fold in egg white mixture.

4. Divide batter evenly between lined muffin tins, filling each a little over half full. Bake until cake tester inserted in centers comes out clean, about 18 minutes. Rotate tins halfway through the baking process to promote even baking. Remove from oven and cool in the pan for 5 minutes. Transfer cupcakes to wire racks to cool completely.

For Buttercream Frosting:

1. In a small mixing bowl, cream butter and sugar together. Add orange juice, vanilla, orange zest and milk, beat until light and smooth.

2. Using a small offset spatula, generously frost each cupcake. Serve.

Raspberry-Jam Cupcakes

PREP TIME: 15 min
BAKING TIME: 20–25 min

makes 16 cupcakes

INGREDIENTS

3 cups (750 ml) unbleached all-purpose flour

1 teaspoon baking powder

½ teaspoon kosher salt

1 cup (250 ml) unsalted butter, room temperature (2 sticks)

1½ cups (350 ml) granulated sugar

4 fresh large eggs, separated, room temperature

½ cup (125 ml) milk

1 cup (250 ml) raspberry jam or preserves

FOR MILK GLAZE:

1½ cups (350 ml) confectioners' sugar, sifted

3 tablespoons milk

METHOD

1. Preheat oven to 350°F (177°C). Spray muffin tins with nonstick cooking spray. In a medium bowl, whisk flour, baking powder and salt together.

2. In a large bowl, using an electric mixer on medium-high speed, cream butter and sugar until light and fluffy. Add egg yolks, one at a time, beating until each one is combined. Scrape down the sides of the bowl as necessary. Reduce speed to low. Add flour mixture in three batches, alternating with the milk, and beating until just combined.

3. In a separate bowl, with an electric mixer on medium speed, beat egg whites until soft peaks form. Gently fold into batter. Spoon 2 tablespoons batter into each muffin cup. Make an indentation in the middle of each and spoon 1 tablespoon of jam on top of the batter. Top with 2 tablespoons of batter, completely covering the jam.

4. Bake for about 20 to 25 minutes or until a cake tester inserted in the middle comes out clean. Rotate tins halfway through the baking process to promote even baking. Remove from oven. Run a small offset spatula around the edges of the cupcakes, and turn out onto wire racks. Let cool completely before adding glaze.

For Milk Glaze:

Whisk confectioners' sugar and milk together until smooth. Use immediately.

Apple Crisp Cinnamon Swirl Cupcakes

PREP TIME: 15 min
BAKING TIME: 25 min

makes 12 cupcakes

INGREDIENTS

For Swirl and Topping:

½ cup (125 ml) granulated sugar

2 tablespoons ground cinnamon

1 large apple, peeled and grated

2 tablespoons cinnamon sugar swirl

1¼ cups (300 ml) all-purpose flour

¾ cup (175 ml) granulated sugar

¾ teaspoon baking soda

¼ teaspoon kosher salt

2 fresh large eggs

1 cup (250 ml) canola oil

1 teaspoon pure vanilla extract

3 tablespoons unsalted butter, melted

METHOD

1. Position rack in the middle of the oven. Preheat oven to 350°F (177°C). Line muffin tins with paper or foil cupcake liners. In a small bowl, mix the sugar and cinnamon together to make the cinnamon sugar for the swirl and topping. Set aside.

2. In a separate bowl, mix the grated apple with 2 tablespoons of cinnamon sugar. Set aside. In a large bowl, mix the flour, sugar, baking soda and salt together. Make a well in the center of the flour mixture and add the eggs, oil and vanilla. Stir until everything is smooth and well blended. Stir in the grated apple mixture.

3. Spoon about 2 tablespoons of batter into each lined muffin cup. Sprinkle each cupcake with ½ teaspoon of cinnamon sugar. Spoon the remaining batter over the cinnamon sugar for each cupcake. Using a pastry brush, dab each cupcake with melted butter and sprinkle remaining cinnamon sugar over the top.

4. Bake for about 25 minutes or just until the tops are golden brown, and cake tester inserted in the middle comes out clean. Rotate tins halfway through the baking process to promote even baking. Cool for 15 minutes in the pan on a wire rack. Remove cupcakes from pan and let cool completely.

Pineapple Upside-Down Cupcakes

PREP TIME: 25 min
BAKING TIME: 25–30 min

makes 12 extra-large cupcakes

INGREDIENTS

FOR PINEAPPLE TOPPING:

6 tablespoons unsalted butter, (¾ stick)

2 tablespoons light corn syrup

1 cup (250 ml) packed dark brown sugar

12 pineapple slices, drained (one 20-ounce (600 g) and one 8-ounce (240 g) can)

FOR CUPCAKES:

1¼ cups (300 ml) all-purpose flour

¼ teaspoon baking soda

½ teaspoon baking powder

¼ teaspoon kosher salt

1 fresh large egg

1 fresh large egg yolk

1 cup (250 ml) granulated sugar

½ cup (125 ml) canola oil

1 teaspoon vanilla extract

½ cup (125 ml) sour cream

METHOD

1. Position rack in the middle of the oven. Preheat oven to 350°F (177°C). Line the bottom of extra-large muffin tins with wax paper circles. Spray the wax paper circles and the inside of the muffin tins with nonstick cooking spray.

For Pineapple Topping:

In a medium saucepan over medium heat, combine butter, corn syrup and brown sugar. Stirring continuously, cook until the butter and sugar melt and the mixture is smooth. Remove from heat and set aside.

For Cupcakes:

1. Sift the first four ingredients together in a medium bowl and set aside.

2. In a large bowl, with your electric mixer on medium speed, beat the egg, egg yolk and sugar together until thickened and pale, about 2 to 3 minutes. Scrape the sides of the bowl as needed during mixing. Reduce the mixer speed to low, mixing in the oil and vanilla until combined. Mix in the sour cream and mix until fully incorporated. Mix in the flour mixture and beat until batter is smooth.

3. Put 1 tablespoon plus 1 teaspoon of the brown sugar glaze in the bottom of each prepared muffin cup. Place a slice of pineapple on top of the glaze. Spoon ⅓ cup (75 ml) of batter over each pineapple slice; the batter should come to the top of each cup.

4. Bake for 25 to 30 minutes or just until the tops feel firm, and cake tester inserted in the middle comes out clean. Rotate tins halfway through the baking process to promote even baking. Cool for 5 minutes in the pan on a wire rack. Use a small knife to loosen any tops that may have stuck to the pan. Carefully place a wire rack on top of the cupcakes. Holding the pan and rack together, invert the cupcakes to release them onto the wire rack. Allow to cool completely upside down. Serve.

Blueberry Cupcakes with Whipped Cream Frosting

PREP TIME: 25 min
BAKING TIME: 20-25 min

makes 30 cupcakes

INGREDIENTS

1½ cups (350 ml) unbleached all-purpose flour

1½ cups (350 ml) cake flour, sifted

1 tablespoon baking powder

1 pinch salt

1 cup (250 ml) unsalted butter, room temperature (2 sticks)

1¾ cups granulated sugar

4 fresh large eggs, room temperature

1½ teaspoons pure vanilla extract

1¼ cups (300 ml) milk

2 cups (500 ml) fresh blueberries; plus extra for garnish

For Whipped Cream:

2 cups (500 ml) heavy whipping cream

½ cup (125 ml) confectioners' sugar

½ teaspoon pure vanilla extract

METHOD:

1. Preheat oven to 350°F (177°C). Line muffin tins with paper or foil liners. In a medium bowl sift flours, baking powder and salt together.

2. Using an electric mixer set on medium-high speed, cream butter and sugar together until light and fluffy. Add eggs, one at a time, beating until each is fully incorporated. Scrape the sides of the bowl as necessary. Beat in vanilla extract.

3. Reduce speed to low and add flour mixture, in two batches, alternating with the milk. Beat until thoroughly mixed. Fold in blueberries by hand.

4. Divide batter evenly between lined tins, filling each tin three-quarters full. Bake for about 20 to 25 minutes or until a cake tester inserted in the middle comes out clean. Rotate tins halfway through the baking process to promote even baking. Transfer pans to wire rack to cool completely before removing cupcakes.

For Whipped Cream:

Whip heavy cream until peaks form. Add confectioners' sugar and vanilla, whisk until combined. Spoon whipped cream onto cupcakes. Garnish with fresh blueberies. Serve immediately.

Classics

Black and White Cupcakes

PREP TIME: 25 min
BAKING TIME: 20-25 min

makes 12 cupcakes

INGREDIENTS

3 large fresh eggs, room temperature

1 teaspoon pure vanilla extract

1 teaspoon lemon peel, grated

1½ cups (350 ml) cake flour, sifted

¾ teaspoon baking powder

1 pinch kosher salt

1¼ cups (300 ml) granulated sugar

¾ cup (175 ml) unsalted butter, room temperature (1½ sticks)

⅓ cup (75 ml) buttermilk

FOR CHOCOLATE ICING:

¼ cup (60 m) heavy whipping cream

1 tablespoon light corn syrup

4 ounces (120 g) semisweet chocolate, chopped

½ teaspoon pure vanilla extract

FOR WHITE ICING:

1 cup (250 ml) powdered sugar

2 tablespoons heavy whipping cream

2 teaspoons fresh lemon juice

METHOD

For Cupcakes:

1. Preheat oven to 325°F (163°C). Line muffin tins with paper or foil liners. In a medium bowl, whisk eggs, vanilla and lemon peel to combine. In a separate bowl, mix cake flour, baking powder and salt. Using an electric mixer, beat sugar and butter in large bowl, mixing well. Scraping down sides of bowl as necessary. Gradually beat in egg mixture. Beat in dry ingredients; alternating with buttermilk in 2 portions.

2. Divide batter evenly between prepared muffin tins, filling each tin about three quarters full. Bake for about 20 to 25 minutes or until a cake tester inserted in the middle comes out clean. Rotate tins halfway through the baking process to promote even baking. Cool for 5 minutes in pan on a wire rack. Remove cupcakes from pan and let cool completely.

For Chocolate Icing:

Bring cream and corn syrup to a simmer in small heavy saucepan over medium heat. Remove from heat. Add chocolate and vanilla; whisk until melted and smooth.

For White Icing:

Whisk all ingredients together in a small bowl.

For Chocolate and White Icing:

Let both icings cool and thicken before applying to cupcakes (about 30-45 minutes).

To Assemble:

Spread chocolate icing over half of each cupcake. Spread white icing on the remaining half of each cupcake. Let stand until set, about 1 hour.

■ TIP

Can be made 1 day ahead. Store in an airtight container at room temperature in a single layer.

Carrot Cupcakes with Cream Cheese Frosting

PREP TIME: 20 min
BAKING TIME: 24-28 min

---

makes 30 cupcakes

INGREDIENTS

1 pound (450 g) carrots, peeled and finely grated

3 large eggs, room temperature

2 cups (500 ml) sugar

1/3 cup (75 ml) buttermilk

1 1/2 cups (350 ml) vegetable oil

1 1/2 teaspoons pure vanilla extract

1/2 cup (125 ml) golden raisins

3 cups (750 ml) unbleached all-purpose flour

1 teaspoon kosher salt

1 teaspoon baking soda

2 teaspoons baking powder

1 teaspoon ground ginger

1 teaspoon ground cinnamon

1/8 teaspoon ground cloves

1/2 cup (125 ml) walnuts, coarsely chopped; plus extra for sprinkling

FOR CREAM CHEESE FROSTING:

1 cup (250 ml) unsalted butter, room temperature (2 sticks)

12 ounces (360 g) cream cheese, room temperature

4 cups (1 L) confectioners' sugar

1/2 teaspoon pure vanilla extract

METHOD

1. Preheat oven to 325°F (163°C). Line muffin tins with paper or foil liners.

2. In a mixing bowl, whisk carrots, eggs, sugar, buttermilk, oil, vanilla extract and raisins together. In a separate bowl, whisk together flour, salt, baking soda, baking powder, ginger, cinnamon, cloves and walnuts. Gradually add flour mixture to carrot mixture, stirring until well combined, scraping the sides of the bowl as necessary.

3. Divide batter between lined muffin tins, filling them three-quarters full. Bake until cake tester inserted in centers comes out clean, about 24 to 28 minutes. Rotate tins halfway through the baking process to promote even baking. Remove from oven, transfer to wire racks and cool for about 10 minutes. Remove cupcakes from tins and let cool completely.

For Cream Cheese Frosting:

1. Using an electric mixer on medium-high speed, beat butter and cream cheese together until light and fluffy, about 3 minutes. Reduce speed to low. Gradually, add sugar 1/2 cup (125 ml) at a time. Add vanilla, and mix until texture is smooth, scraping down the sides of the bowl as necessary.

2. Using a small offset spatula spread frosting on cupcakes. Sprinkle chopped walnuts over the tops. Serve.

■ TIP

Frosting may be stored in an air tight container for up to three days. Before using, bring to room temperature and beat on low speed until smooth and fluffy.

Brown Sugar Pound Cupcakes

PREP TIME: 20 min
BAKING TIME: 20–25 min

---

makes 26 cupcakes

INGREDIENTS

3 cups (750 ml) unbleached all-purpose flour, sifted

2 teaspoons baking powder

½ teaspoon salt

1 cup (250 ml) unsalted butter, softened (2 sticks)

2¼ cups (500 ml) light-brown sugar, packed

4 fresh large eggs, room temperature

¾ cup (175 ml) buttermilk

FOR BROWN-SUGAR CREAM-CHEESE FROSTING:

½ cup (125 ml) unsalted butter, softened (1 stick)

8 ounces (240 g) cream cheese, room temperature

1 cup (250 ml) light-brown sugar, packed

METHOD

1. Preheat oven to 325°F (163°C). Line muffin tins with paper or foil liners. In a medium bowl, whisk together flour, baking powder and salt. Set aside.

2. In a large bowl, using an electric mixer set on medium-high speed, cream butter and brown sugar together until light and fluffy. Add eggs, one at a time, beating until well blended. Add flour in three batches, alternating with buttermilk, beating after each new addition.

3. Divide batter between lined muffin tins, filling each three-quarters full. Bake until golden brown and a cake tester inserted in centers comes out clean, about 20 to 25 minutes. Rotate tins halfway through the baking process to promote even baking. Remove from oven, cool cupcakes in the pan on wire racks for 10 minutes. Transfer cupcakes to wire racks and let cool completely before frosting.

For Brown-Sugar Cream-Cheese Frosting:

1. In a medium bowl, using an electric mixer set on medium-high speed, beat butter, cream cheese and brown sugar until creamy and smooth. Use immediately or refrigerate in an airtight container for up to three days. If not using immediately, bring to room temperature and beat on low speed until smooth and creamy.

2. To finish, using an offset spatula, frost each cupcake top with frosting. Serve.

Cheesecake Cupcakes

PREP TIME: 15 min
BAKING TIME: 15 min

makes 24 cupcakes

INGREDIENTS

16 ounces (480 g) cream cheese, room temperature

¾ cup (175 ml) granulated sugar

1 tablespoon pure vanilla extract

2 fresh eggs

1¼ cups (300 ml) graham cracker crumbs

3 tablespoons sugar

½ cup (125 ml) butter, melted (1 stick)

Strawberry, blueberry or cherry pie filling (optional)

METHOD

1. Preheat oven to 350°F (177°C). Line muffin tins with paper or foil liners. In a medium bowl, using an electric mixer at high spped, blend the first four ingredients until smooth and creamy.

2. Mix graham cracker crumbs and sugar in small bowl. Add melted butter and mix to combine. Cool.

3. Place 2 tablespoons of graham cracker crumb mixture in each paper cup and press firmly. Add filling and bake for 8 minutes and cool completely before serving. Top with strawberry, blueberry or cherry pie filling, if desired.

Black Forest Cupcakes

PREP TIME: 20 min
BAKING TIME: 20-30 min

makes 12 cupcakes

INGREDIENTS

2 cups (500 ml) maraschino cherries; plus 12 for garnish, stems intact

¼ cup (60 ml) kirsch (or 2 teaspoons pure vanilla extract for kid-friendly version)

¾ cup (175 ml) water

¾ cup (175 ml) semisweet chocolate chips

1 cup (250 ml) unsalted butter, room temperature (2 sticks)

1 cup (250 ml) packed brown sugar

3 fresh eggs

2½ cups (625 ml) cake flour, sifted

1½ teaspoons baking powder

1½ teaspoons baking soda

¼ teaspoon kosher salt

⅔ cup (150 ml) sour cream

FOR WHIPPED CREAM TOPPING:

2 cups (500 ml) heavy whipping cream

3 tablespoons granulated sugar

1 teaspoon pure vanilla extract

12 fresh cherries, to garnish

Chocolate shavings, to garnish

METHOD

1. Preheat oven to 350°F (177°C). Line muffin tins with paper or foil liners.

2. Combine cherry halves with kirsch and set aside. In a small saucepan, over high heat combine water and chocolate chips. Bring to a boil, stirring frequently until chocolate has melted. Remove from heat and allow to cool.

3. In a large bowl, using an electric mixer set on medium speed, cream butter and brown sugar together until light and fluffy. Add eggs, one at a time; add cooled chocolate, scraping the sides of the pan, and mix thoroughly. Whisk together flour, baking powder, baking soda, and salt. Add flour mixture to chocolate mixture in batches, alternating with the sour cream. Mixing on low speed to incorporate.

4. Fill muffin tins half full with batter, add a spoonful of cherries, reserving the liquid and top with batter, so that muffin tins are filled to the rim.

5. Bake for 20 to 30 minutes, until firm to the touch. Cool in the pan for 10 minutes; turn out and cool completely on wire racks.

6. Using a toothpick, poke several holes in the top of the cupcake. Drizzle the reserved cherry liquid over the top of the cupcake; allow liquid to soak in.

For Whipped Cream:

In a large chilled glass or stainless steel bowl, beat heavy cream until soft peaks form. Add sugar and vanilla, beat until incorporated.

To Serve:

Place a dollop of whipped cream on top of each cupcake. Decorate with fresh cherries and shaved chocolate. Refrigerate until ready to serve.

Boston Cream Cupcakes

PREP TIME: 25 min
BAKING TIME: 25 min

makes 18 servings

INGREDIENTS

FOR CREAM FILLING:

2 large egg yolks

¼ cup (60 ml) granulated sugar

2 tablespoons cornstarch

¼ teaspoon kosher salt

1 cup (250 ml) milk

1 teaspoon pure vanilla extract

FOR CUPCAKES:

1½ cups (350 ml) unbleached all-purpose flour

1½ teaspoons baking powder

½ teaspoon kosher salt

½ cup (125 ml) milk

6 tablespoons unsalted butter, room temperature

3 large fresh eggs

1 cup (250 ml) granulated sugar

1 teaspoon pure vanilla extract

FOR CHOCOLATE GLAZE:

⅔ cup (150 ml) heavy whipping cream

6 ounces (180 g) semisweet chocolate, finely chopped

1 tablespoon light corn syrup

METHOD

For Cream Filling:

1. Whisk egg yolks until smooth. Set aside. Combine sugar, cornstarch and salt in a saucepan over medium heat; stir well. Gradually add milk; stir with a wire whisk until blended. Bring to a boil, cook until thick; about 5 minutes, stirring constantly.

2. Remove from heat. Gradually stir one-fourth of hot milk mixture into eggs to temper them; now add egg mixture to remaining milk mixture, stirring constantly. Cook over medium heat, stirring constantly, about 2 to 4 minutes or until thickened. Stir in vanilla and remove from heat. Pour mixture into a bowl; place plastic wrap on surface of pastry cream, and chill for at least 1 hour (can be stored in the refrigerator for up to 2 days).

For Cupcakes:

1. Preheat oven to 350°F (177°C). Spray muffin tins with nonstick cooking spray.

2. In a small bowl, whisk together flour, baking powder and salt. Combine milk and butter in a saucepan, set over low heat.

3. Using an electric mixer on high speed, beat eggs and sugar until fluffy and pale, about 5 minutes. Reduce mixer speed to medium and gradually beat in dry ingredients.

4. Bring milk and butter to a boil. With mixer on low speed, add milk mixture to batter; beat until smooth and creamy. Add vanilla (do not overmix).

5. Divide batter evenly between muffin tins, filling each halfway. Bake until cupcakes are light gold and a cake tester inserted in the center comes out clean; about 25 minutes. Rotate tins halfway through the baking process, to promote even baking. Remove from oven; cool in tins for 10 minutes. Run a knife around the edges to loosen; transfer cupcakes to wire racks to cool completely.

For Chocolate Glaze:

Bring cream to a boil in small saucepan over medium-high heat. Remove from heat; add chocolate and corn syrup. Let rest for 5 to 7 minutes. Stir until smooth. Let glaze cool in a bowl, stirring frequently.

Assembly:

1. Fill a pastry bag with vanilla cream; remove a cone-shaped section from center of each cupcake, fill hole with vanilla cream and then replace the top of the cake piece.

2. Drizzle or spoon chocolate glaze over top of each cupcake. Serve.

Snickerdoodle Cupcakes

PREP TIME: 15 min
BAKING TIME: 20 min

makes 28 cupcakes

INGREDIENTS

1½ cups (350 ml) unbleached all-purpose flour

1½ cups (350 m) cake flour, sifted

1 tablespoon baking powder

½ teaspoon salt

1 tablespoon ground cinnamon, plus ¼ teaspoon for dusting

1 cup (250 ml) unsalted butter, room temperature (2 sticks)

1¾ cups (400 ml) granulated sugar, plus 1½ tablespoons for dusting

4 fresh large eggs, room temperature

2 teaspoons pure vanilla extract

1¼ cups (300 ml) milk

FOR SEVEN-MINUTE FROSTING:

2 cups (500 ml) granulated sugar

3 large egg whites

3 tablespoons light corn syrup

3 tablespoons cold water

1 teaspoon pure vanilla extract

METHOD

1. Preheat oven to 350°F (177°C). Line muffin tins with paper or foil liners.

2. In a mixing bowl, sift together flours, baking powder, salt and 1 tablespoon cinnamon.

3. In a large mixing bowl, with an electric mixer on medium-high speed, cream butter and sugar until light and fluffy. Beat in eggs, one at a time, beating until each is combined, scraping down the sides of the bowl as necessary. Beat in the vanilla. Reduce speed; add flour mixture in three batches, alternating with milk, beating until completely combined.

4. Divide batter between lined muffin tins, filling each three-quarters full. Bake until cake tester inserted in centers comes out clean, about 20 minutes. Rotate tins halfway through the baking process to promote even baking. Remove from oven, transfer tins to wire racks to cool completely before removing cupcakes.

For Seven-Minute Frosting:

1. Using the top of a double boiler combine sugar, egg whites, corn syrup, water and vanilla. Place over boiling water and beat with an electric mixer on high speed until peaks form, or for 7 minutes. Remove from heat.

2. Using a pastry bag fitted with a large plain tip, pipe frosting on each cupcake. Combine ¼ teaspoon cinnamon and 1½ tablespoons sugar. Using a fine, small sieve, lightly dust frosted cupcakes with cinnamon sugar. Serve.

Chocolate Truffle Cupcakes

PREP TIME: 45 min
CHILLING TIME: 4 h
BAKING TIME: 15–18 min

---

makes 12 cupcakes

INGREDIENTS

FOR CHOCOLATE TRUFFLES:

5 ounces (150 g) bittersweet chocolate, coarsely chopped

¼ cup (60 ml) heavy cream

2 tablespoons Cognac

FOR CHOCOLATE CAKE:

9 ounces (270 g) bittersweet chocolate, finely chopped

1 cup plus 2 tablespoons (280 ml) unsalted butter (2¼ sticks)

5 large eggs

1 cup plus 1 tablespoon (265 ml) granulated sugar

½ cup (125 ml) cornstarch, sifted

1 teaspoon pure vanilla extract

METHOD

For the Truffles:

1. Melt the chocolate using a double boiler over medium heat. Stirring occasionally until melted, being careful not to burn the chocolate.

2. In a small saucepan bring the cream and Cognac to a boil and whisk the cream mixture into the chocolate until smooth. Cover the bowl with plastic wrap and refrigerate for at least 4 hours or overnight until set.

3. Once the mixture has set, remove from the refrigerator and form into twelve ½-inch (1½ cm) balls. Flatten the truffles slightly into discs and refrigerate until ready to use.

For Chocolate Cake:

1. Position oven rack in the center of the oven and preheat to 325ºF (163ºC). Butter and sugar the bottom and sides of standard size muffin tins.

2. Melt the chocolate and butter in a double boiler over medium heat; set aside to cool.

3. In a separate medium bowl, whisk together the eggs and sugar until light in color and fluffy. Whisk the cooled chocolate mixture into the egg mixture and then gently fold in the cornstarch and vanilla.

4. Fill each of the prepared muffin tins one-third full. Place a truffle into the center of each cupcake and cover with the remaining batter filling the the cup two-thirds full.

5. Bake the cupcakes for 15 to 18 minutes or until the cake has formed a crust and is soft to the touch. Place the cupcakes on a wire rack and allow to cool for 5 minutes. Serve immediately.

Coconut Cupcakes with Seven-Minute Frosting

PREP TIME: 25 min
BAKING TIME: 20 min

---

makes 20 cupcakes

INGREDIENTS

1¾ cups (400 ml) unbleached all-purpose flour

½ teaspoon salt

2 teaspoons baking powder

½ cup (125 ml) sweetened shredded coconut

¾ cup (175 ml) unsalted butter, room temperature (1½ sticks)

1⅓ cups (300 ml) granulated sugar

4 extra-large eggs, room temperature

1½ teaspoons pure almond extract

1½ teaspoons pure vanilla extract

¾ cup (175 ml) buttermilk

1½ cups (350 ml) sweetened flaked coconut, for garnish

FOR SEVEN-MINUTE FROSTING:

2 cups (500 ml) granulated sugar

3 large egg whites

3 tablespoons light corn syrup

3 tablespoons cold water

1 teaspoon pure vanilla extract

METHOD

1. Preheat oven to 350°F (177°C). Line muffins tins with paper liners.

2. In a mixing bowl, whisk together flour, salt and baking powder. Using a food processor, pulse shredded coconut until finely ground; whisk into flour mixture.

3. In a large mixing bowl, with an electric mixer on medium-high speed, cream butter and sugar until light and fluffy. Gradually beat in eggs, almond and vanilla extract, scraping the sides of bowl as necessary. Reduce speed; add flour mixture in thirds, alternating with buttermilk, beating until completely combined.

4. Divide batter between lined muffin tins, filling them three-quarters full. Bake until cake tester inserted in centers comes out clean, about 20 minutes. Rotate tins halfway through the baking process to promote even baking. Remove from oven, transfer to wire racks and cool completely.

For Seven-Minute Frosting:

1. Using the top of a double boiler combine sugar, egg whites, corn syrup, water and vanilla. Place over boiling water and beat with an electric mixer on high speed until peaks form, or for 7 minutes. Remove from heat.

2. Using a small offset spatula, generously frost each cupcake. Garnish with flaked coconut. Serve.

■ **TIP**

Cupcakes are best eaten the day they are frosted.

Red Velvet Cupcakes with Cream Cheese Frosting

PREP TIME: 25 min
BAKING TIME: 20 min

makes 24 cupcakes

INGREDIENTS

2½ cups (600 ml) cake flour, not self-rising

2 tablespoons unsweetened cocoa powder

1 teaspoon salt

1½ cups (350 ml) sugar

1½ cups (350 ml) vegetable oil

2 eggs

1 teaspoon red gel-paste food coloring

1 teaspoon pure vanilla extract

1 cup (250 ml) buttermilk

1½ teaspoons baking soda

2 teaspoons white vinegar

FOR CREAM CHEESE FROSTING:

1 cup (250 ml) unsalted butter, room temperature (2 sticks)

12 ounces (360 g) cream cheese, room temperature

4 cups (1 L) confectioners' sugar

½ teaspoon pure vanilla extract

METHOD

1. Preheat oven to 350°F (177°C). Line muffins tins with paper liners.

2. Sift cake flour into a mixing bowl, add cocoa and salt. Set aside. Using an electric mixer set on medium-high speed, whisk sugar and oil together until combined. Add eggs, one at a time, beating until incorporated, scraping the sides of the bowl occasionally. Mix in food coloring and vanilla.

3. Reduce speed to low. Gradually add flour mixture in three batches, alternating with the buttermilk. Whisk well to combine. In a small bowl, stir together baking soda and vinegar, and add to batter. Mix on medium speed for 15 seconds.

4. Divide batter among lined tins, filling each one three-quarters full. Bake, rotating tins halfway through the baking process, for about 20 minutes or until a cake tester inserted in centers comes out clean.

5. Transfer tins to wire racks to cool completely before removing cupcakes and decorating.

For Cream Cheese Frosting:

1. Using an electric mixer on medium-high speed, beat butter and cream cheese together until light and fluffy, about 3 minutes. Reduce speed to low. Gradually, add sugar ½ cup (125 ml) at a time. Add vanilla and mix until texture is smooth, scraping down the sides of the bowl as necessary.

2. Using a small offset spatula spread frosting on cupcakes.

◼ TIP

Frosting may be stored in an air tight container for up to three days. Before using, bring to room temperature and beat on low speed until smooth and fluffy.

Yellow Buttermilk Cupcakes with Vanilla Frosting

PREP TIME: 25 min
BAKING TIME: 18–20 min

---

makes 36 cupcakes

INGREDIENTS

1½ cups (350 ml) unbleached all-purpose flour

3 cups (750 ml) cake flour (not self-rising)

¾ teaspoon baking soda

2 teaspoons baking powder

1 teaspoon kosher salt

1 cup plus 2 tablespoons (280 ml) unsalted butter, room temperature (2¼ sticks)

2¼ cups (560 ml) granulated sugar

5 fresh large whole eggs, room temperature

3 fresh egg yolks, room temperature

2 cups (500 ml) buttermilk, room temperature

2 teaspoons pure vanilla extract

FOR VANILLA FROSTING:

1½ cups (350 ml) unsalted butter, room temperature (3 sticks)

4 cups (1 L) confectioners' sugar, sifted

1 teaspoon pure vanilla extract

METHOD

1. Preheat oven to 350°F (177°C). Line muffin tins with paper or foil liners. In a medium bowl sift flours, baking soda, baking powder and salt together.

2. Using an electric mixer set on medium-high speed, cream butter and sugar together until light and fluffy. Reduce speed to medium. Add whole eggs, one at a time, beating until each is fully incorporated. Scrape the sides of the bowl as necessary. Add egg yolks and mix well. Reduce speed to low; add flour mixture, in two batches, alternating with the buttermilk. Beat until thoroughly mixed. Beat in vanilla.

3. Divide batter evenly between lined tins, filling each cup three-quarters full. Bake for 18 to 20 minutes or until a cake tester inserted in the middle comes out clean. Rotate tins halfway through the baking process to promote even baking. Cool for 15 minutes in pan on a wire rack. Remove cupcakes from pan. Cool completely on wire racks before frosting.

For Vanilla Frosting:

1. Using an electric mixer on medium-high speed, beat butter until light and creamy, about 2 to 3 minutes. Reduce speed to medium and gradually add confectioners' sugar, beating well as you add. Scrape down the sides of the bowl as necessary. Beat for about 5 minutes, or until frosting is light and airy. Add vanilla and beat until frosting is creamy.

2. Using a small offset spatula, spread frosting over the tops of the cupcakes.

■ TIP

Store in the refrigerator in an airtight container for up to 3 days.

Holiday/
Seasonal

Easter Coconut Nest Cupcakes

PREP TIME: 20 min

BAKING TIME: 18 min

---

makes 12 cupcakes

INGREDIENTS

1 cup (250 ml) all-purpose flour

½ teaspoon baking soda

½ teaspoon baking powder

1 pinch kosher salt

¼ cup (60 ml) unsalted butter, softened (½ stick)

¾ cup (175 ml) granulated sugar

2 fresh large eggs

1 teaspoon pure vanilla extract

½ cup (125 ml) buttermilk

FOR CREAM CHEESE FROSTING:

½ cup (125 ml) unsalted butter, softened (1 stick)

4 ounces (120 g) cream cheese, softened

1 teaspoon pure vanilla extract

2 cups (500 ml) confectioners' sugar

2 cups (500 ml) shredded sweetened coconut

36 jelly beans, pastel-colored

METHOD

1. Place oven rack in the middle position in the oven. Preheat oven to 350°F (177°C). Line muffin tins with paper or foil liners.

2. In a medium bowl, sift together flour, baking soda, baking powder and salt. Set aside

3. In a large bowl, using an electric mixer on medium speed, cream the butter and sugar together until light and creamy, about 1 minute. Scrape the sides of the bowl as necessary. Add the eggs one at a time, beating mixture until creamy. Mix in the vanilla. Reduce mixer speed to low, add half of the flour mixture, mixing until just incorporated. Mix in the buttermilk, followed by the remaining flour mixture until batter looks smooth and creamy.

4. Divide batter between lined muffin tins, filling them three-quarters full. Bake until the tops feel firm and a cake tester inserted in the center comes out clean, about 18 minutes. Rotate tins halfway through the baking process to promote even baking. Remove from oven, transfer pans to a wire rack and cool for about 10 minutes. Remove cupcakes from pan and cool completely on wire rack.

For Cream Cheese Frosting:

1. In a large bowl, using an electric mixer set on low speed, beat butter, cream cheese and vanilla together until smooth and creamy, about one minute. Scrape down the sides of the bowl as necessary. Add the confectioners' sugar, mixing on medium speed until light and creamy.

2. Using a spatula, spread about 3 tablespoons of frosting evenly over the top on each cupcake. Sprinkle the coconut generously over the frosting, leave a small space in the center that is lightly covered. Arrange 3 jelly beans in the center of the frosted cupcake to resemble eggs in a nest. Store covered in the refrigerator. Serve.

Ice Cream Bon-bon Mini-Cupcakes

PREP TIME: 30 min
CHILLING TIME: 1 h

---

makes 36 cupcakes

INGREDIENTS

12 ounces (360 g) semisweet or bittersweet chocolate, chopped

3 pints (1½ L) ice cream, softened until just spreadable

METHOD

1. Line mini-muffin tins with mini paper or foil liners (use two liners for each cupcake).

2. Place chocolate in the top of a double boiler or in a heatproof bowl. Place over a saucepan of barely simmering water. Stir the chocolate until it is melted and smooth. Remove pan or bowl from water.

3. Put about 1½ teaspoons of the melted chocolate in the paper liner, using a pastry brush no wider than 1-inch, brush the chocolate up the sides of the liner almost to the top, completely coating the paper liner. Repeat this until all of the chocolate is gone. Put chocolate cups on a baking sheet and freeze for at least 1 hour or overnight.

4. Using a small spoon, fill chocolate cups with about 2 tablespoons of ice cream, gently pressing the ice cream into the cup and mounding it above the rim. Place on baking sheet and freeze until firm.

5. Once the ice cream is firm, peel the paper liners away from the chocolate and place each cupcake in a clean paper liner. Serve.

■ TIP

If not using immediately, wrap individually in plastic wrap and return to freezer. Can be frozen for up to one week.

Fourth of July Cupcakes

PREP TIME: 20 min
BAKING TIME: 20-25 min

makes 36 cupcakes

INGREDIENTS

¾ cup (175 ml) unsweetened Dutch-processed cocoa powder

¾ cup (175 ml) hot water

3 cups (750 ml) unbleached all-purpose flour

1 teaspoon baking powder

1 teaspoon baking soda

1¼ teaspoons kosher salt

1½ cups (350 ml) unsalted butter (3 sticks)

2¼ cups (500 ml) granulated sugar

4 large fresh eggs, at room temperature

1 tablespoon pure vanilla extract

1 cup (250 ml) sour cream, at room temperature

FOR FROSTING:

2 cups (500 m) heavy whipping cream

¼ cup (60 ml) confectioners' sugar

1 teaspoon pure vanilla extract

32 fresh strawberries, rinsed; dried; hulled and halved

1½ cups (350 ml) fresh blueberries

METHOD

1. Preheat oven to 350°F (177°C). Line muffin tins with paper or foil liners.

2. In a small bowl, whisk together cocoa and hot water until well mixed and smooth. In a separate bowl, whisk together flour, baking powder, baking soda and salt. Set aside.

3. In a saucepan over medium-low heat, melt butter with sugar, stirring constantly to combine. Remove from heat; pour into a large mixing bowl. Using an electric mixer on medium-low speed, beat for 4 or 5 minutes. Add eggs, 1 at a time, beating until incorporated. Add vanilla and cocoa mixture, and beat until blended. Reduce mixer speed to low. Gradually add flour mixture in two batches, alternating with sour cream. Beat until just combined.

4. Divide batter between lined muffin tins, filling them three-quarters full. Bake until cake tester inserted in centers comes out clean, about 20 minutes. Rotate tins halfway through the baking process, to promote even baking. Remove from oven; cool in pan on wire rack for 15 minutes. Remove cupcakes from pan and let cool completely.

For Whipped Cream Frosting:

In a large glass or stainless steel bowl, beat heavy cream until soft peaks form. Add confectioners' sugar and vanilla, beat until incorporated.

To Serve:

Place a dollop of whipped cream on top of each cupcake. Decorate with fresh strawberries and blueberries. Serve.

■ TIP

Cupcakes can be frozen in an airtight container for up to 2 months (unfrosted).

Halloween Cupcakes

PREP TIME: 20 min
BAKING TIME: 20-25 min

makes 12 cupcakes

INGREDIENTS

1½ cups (350 ml) unbleached
all-purpose flour

1½ teaspoons baking powder

¼ teaspoon salt

2 large eggs, at room temperature

¾ cup butter (175 m), room temperature
(1½ sticks)

⅔ cup (150 ml) sugar

1 teaspoon vanilla extract

FOR FROSTING:

8 ounces (240 g) store-bought vanilla
frosting

Orange food coloring, (or red and
yellow)

Sprinkles

M&M's or Reese's Pieces candies

METHOD

1. Preheat the oven to 350°F (177°C). Line muffin tins with paper liners.

2. In a mixing bowl, whisk flour, baking powder and salt together.

3. In a separate bowl, beat the eggs, butter and sugar with an electric mixer until light in color. Add vanilla extract and beat until blended. Mix in half of the dry ingredients by hand, being careful not to over mix. Add the remaining dry ingredients and mix.

4. Divide batter between lined muffin tins, filling them three-quarters full. Bake until cake tester inserted in centers comes out clean, about 20 to 25 minutes. Remove from oven; cool in the pan for 10 minutes. Transfer cupcakes to wire racks and cool completely before frosting.

For Frosting:

Mix the frosting with the food coloring until desired shade of orange is reached. Frost cupcakes. Decorate with sprinkles and candies or plastic spiders, if preferred.

Pumpkin Cupcakes with Cream Cheese Frosting

PREP TIME: 25 min
BAKING TIME: 18-20 min

makes 12 cupcakes

INGREDIENTS

1½ cups (350 ml) unbleached all-purpose flour

1 teaspoon baking soda

1 teaspoon ground cinnamon

¼ teaspoon ground cloves

¼ teaspoon ground ginger

½ teaspoon kosher salt

½ cup (125 ml) unsalted butter, softened (1 stick)

1 cup (250 ml) granulated sugar

2 fresh large eggs

1 teaspoon pure vanilla extract

¾ cup (175 ml) canned pumpkin puree, solid packed

FOR CREAM CHEESE FROSTING:

8 ounces (240 g) cream cheese; softened

4 tablespoons unsalted butter, softened

1 teaspoon pure vanilla extract

3 cups (750 ml) confectioners' sugar; sifted

1½ cups (350 ml) English toffee bits

METHOD

1. Position oven rack in the middle position. Preheat oven to 350°F (177°C). Line muffin tins with paper or foil liners.

2. In a large bowl, sift flour, baking soda, spices and salt together. In a separate bowl, using an electric mixer set on medium-high speed, cream the butter and sugar together until light and fluffy. Add the eggs, one at a time, beating well. Beat in the vanilla, scraping down the sides of the bowl as necessary. With the mixer on low speed, add the flour mixture and pumpkin puree, in three additions, alternating between the two, beginning and ending with the flour mixture.

3. Divide batter among lined tins, filling each one three-quarters full. Bake, rotating tins halfway through the baking process, for about 18 to 20 minutes or until a cake tester inserted in centers comes out clean. Cool completely on a wire rack before frosting.

For Cream Cheese Frosting:

1. With your electric mixer set on medium, beat cream cheese until smooth and creamy. Add the butter and beat until fully incorporated. Add confectoners' sugar and vanilla and beat until light and fluffy, about 2 to 3 minutes. Pipe or spread frosting on the cupcakes.

2. Sprinkle tops of frosted cupcakes with toffee bits. Serve.

Tiramisu Cupcakes

PREP TIME: 35 min
BAKING TIME: 15 min
CHILLING TIME: 8 h

makes 18 cupcakes

INGREDIENTS

1 cup (250 ml) unbleached all-purpose flour

¾ teaspoon baking powder

¼ teaspoon kosher salt

4 fresh large eggs, room temperature

⅔ cup (150 ml) granulated sugar

1¼ teaspoons pure vanilla extract

FOR SYRUP:

½ cup (125 ml) water

⅓ cup (75 ml) sugar

2 tablespoons marsala

2 teaspoons instant espresso powder

FOR FILLING:

8 ounces (240 g) mascarpone cheese, room temperature

½ cup (125 ml) confectioners' sugar

1 tablespoon marsala

¾ cup (175 ml) heavy whipping cream, chilled

Cocoa powder, for dusting

METHOD

1. Preheat oven to 350°F (177°C). Line muffin tins with paper or foil liners.

2. In a medium bowl, whisk together flour, baking powder and salt. In a large bowl, using an electric mixer set on medium-high speed, beat the eggs for about 3 minutes. Add the sugar and vanilla, and continue beating until mixture has tripled in volume, or about 3 minutes more. Using a rubber spatula, gradually add the flour mixture over the egg mixture. Gently fold until fully blended.

3. Divide batter between lined muffin tins, filling them three-quarters full. Bake until cake tester inserted in centers comes out clean, about 15 minutes. Rotate tins halfway through the baking process, to promote even baking. Remove from oven, transfer tins to wire racks and cool completely.

For Syrup:

In a small saucepan, over medium heat, combine the water and sugar, stirring often until sugar is completely dissolved. Bring to a quick boil and remove from heat. Stir in the marsala and espresso powder. Set aside and cool to room temperature. Once cooled; make slits in the tops of each cupcake with a sharp knife and brush the espresso syrup over the tops, repeat until all the syrup has been used. Let sit for 30 minutes to allow cupcakes to absorb the liquid.

For Mascarpone Cheese Filling:

1. In a medium bowl, using an electric mixer set on medium speed, beat mascarpone, confectioners' sugar and marsala together until well combined. Add the heavy cream and beat for another 2 minutes, or until the filling is fluffy.

2. Spoon filling into a pastry bag, insert tip into the top of the cupcake to squeeze in a small amount. Dollop frosting onto cupcakes; refrigerate 8 hours or overnight in an airtight container. Dust with cocoa powder and serve.

Glazed Orange Cupcakes with Sugared Cranberries

PREP TIME: 30 min
COOKING: 18-20 min
CHILLING: 8 h

makes 12 cupcakes

INGREDIENTS

½ cup (125 ml) unsalted butter, softened (1 stick)

1 cup (250 ml) granulated sugar

2 fresh eggs: room temperature

½ teaspoon pure vanilla extract

2 cups (500 ml) cake flour, sifted before measured

2 teaspoons baking powder

1 pinch salt

½ cup (125 ml) milk

¼ cup (60 ml) orange juice

1 tablespoon orange zest

FOR GLAZE:

1½ cups (350 ml) confectioners' sugar, sifted (plus more if needed)

3 tablespoons fresh orange juice, (plus more if needed)

FOR SUGARED CRANBERRIES:

1 cup (250 ml) granulated sugar

1 cup (250 ml) water

1 cup (250 ml) fresh cranberries

½ cup (125 ml) superfine sugar

METHOD

1. Preheat oven to 375°F. Coat muffin tins with nonstick cooking spray.

2. Using an electric mixer, beat butter and sugar together until light and fluffy. Beat in eggs 1 at a time; add vanilla. Mix sifted flour with baking powder and salt; sift again. Combine milk with orange juice.

3. Working in 2 batches, stir flour mixture and then milk mixture into butter mixture. Stir in zest.

4. Divide batter evenly between prepared muffin tins, filling each three-quarters full. Bake until cake tester inserted in centers comes out clean, about 18 to 20 minutes, or until light golden brown. Rotate tins halfway through the baking process to promote even baking. Remove from oven; cool in pan on wire rack for 15 minutes. Remove cupcakes from pan and let cool completely.

For Glaze:

Whisk sugar and orange juice together until smooth and the desired consistency has been attained. Add more sugar to thicken or more orange juice to thin the glaze. Invert cooled cupcakes and spoon glaze over the top.

For Sugared Cranberries:

1. Combine sugar and water in a small saucepan over low heat. Stir until sugar completely dissolves. Bring to a slow simmer and remove from heat (do not boil, as cranberries will pop). Stir in cranberries and pour into a bowl. Cover and refrigerate for 8 hours or overnight.

2. Drain cranberries in a colander. Place superfine sugar in a shallow pan or dish. Add the cranberries to the sugar, rolling to fully coat. Line a baking sheet with parchment paper. Spread sugared cranberries in a single layer on baking sheet. Let stand at room temperature for at least 1 hour or until dry.

3. Garnish glazed cupcakes with sugared cranberries and serve.

Pink Peppermint Cupcakes

PREP TIME: 20 min
BAKING TIME: 22 min

---

makes 30 cupcakes

INGREDIENTS

1 package white cake mix

1 1/3 cups (300 ml) water

3 fresh egg whites

2 tablespoons butter, melted

1/2 teaspoon peppermint extract

3 drops red food coloring

1 container vanilla frosting, (16 ounces)

1/2 cup (125 ml) hard peppermint candies, crushed (about 16-18 candies)

METHOD

1. Preheat oven to 350°F (177°C). Line muffin tins with paper or foil liners.

2. In a large bowl, with an electric mixer set on low speed, beat cake mix, water, egg whites, butter, peppermint extract, and food coloring, for 30 seconds or until blended. Increase speed to medium and beat for 2 minutes longer, scraping down the sides of the bowl as needed.

3. Divide batter evenly between lined muffin tins, filling them three-quarters full. Bake until cake tester inserted in centers comes out clean, about 20 to 22 minutes. Rotate tins halfway through the baking process to promote even baking. Remove from oven, cool cupcakes in pans on a wire rack for 10 minutes. Remove cupcakes from pans; cool completely on wire racks before frosting.

4. Frost cupcakes tops and sprinkle with crushed peppermints. Serve.

Easy Holiday Cupcakes

PREP TIME: 20 min
BAKING TIME: Per package directions
CHILLING TIME: 30 min

---

makes 24 cupcakes

INGREDIENTS

1 package white cake mix

1 cup (250 ml) boiling water

1 package gelatin (such as JELL-O brand), any red flavor (3-ounce size/ 180 g)

1 tub whipped topping, thawed (8-ounce size/240 g)

Red or green food coloring

Colored sugar for sprinkling

METHOD

1. Prepare and bake cupcake batter as directed on cake mix package. Cool cupcakes in pans on wire racks for 10 minutes. Poke holes in cupcake tops using a fork (meat fork works best).

2. Place gelatin mix in a small bowl, add boiling water, stirring until gelatin is completely dissolved. Spoon gelatin over cupcakes and refrigerate for at least 30 minutes. Remove cupcakes from pan.

3. Divide whipped topping between three bowls, tint one bowl with a drop of red food coloring, and one with green, leave remaining bowl untinted. Spread whipped topping over cupcakes. Decorate with colored sugar. Store in the refrigerator until ready to serve.

Something Special

Iced Coffee Cupcakes

PREP TIME: 20 min
BAKING TIME: 15–20 min

makes 20 cupcakes

INGREDIENTS

1 package chocolate fudge cake mix (without pudding in the mix)

1 package chocolate instant pudding mix (4-serving size)

1⅓ cups (300 ml) brewed coffee, cooled

3 fresh eggs

½ cup (125 ml) vegetable oil

1 teaspoon vanilla

½ gallon (2 L) coffee or mocha ice cream, softened

1 bottle quick-hardening chocolate shell dessert topping

½ cup (125 ml) walnuts or pecans, chopped

METHOD

1. Preheat oven to 350°F (177°C). Line muffin tins with paper or foil liners.

2. In a large bowl, using an electric mixer set on low, beat cake mix, pudding mix, coffee, eggs, oil and vanilla for 1 minute. Beat at medium speed until fluffy, about 2 minutes.

3. Divide batter between lined muffin tins, filling them three-quarters full. Bake until cake tester inserted in centers comes out clean, about 15 to 20 minutes. Rotate tins halfway through the baking process, to promote even baking. Remove from oven, cool in pans on a wire rack for 15 minutes. Remove from pans and cool completely on wire racks.

4. Remove about 1 tablespoon of cake from the center of each cupcake. Fill with 2 to 3 tablespoons softened ice cream, mounding slightly. Drizzle about 1 tablespoon chocolate dessert topping over ice cream, immediately sprinkle with chopped nuts. Place in freezer until ready to serve.

S'mores Cupcakes

PREP TIME: 30 min
BAKING TIME: 25 min

makes 24 cupcakes

INGREDIENTS

1½ cups (350 ml) unbleached all-purpose flour

1⅓ cups (300 ml) graham cracker crumbs

2 teaspoons baking powder

1 teaspoon kosher salt

1½ teaspoons ground cinnamon

1¼ cups (300 ml) unsalted butter, softened (2½ sticks)

2 cups (500 ml) packed light-brown sugar

¼ cup (60 ml) honey

6 fresh large eggs

2 teaspoons pure vanilla extract

FOR CHOCOLATE GANACHE GLAZE:

6 ounces (180 g) semisweet chocolate, finely chopped

⅔ cup (150 ml) heavy whipping cream

1 tablespoon light corn syrup

FOR MARSHMALLOW FROSTING:

1 jar marshmallow creme (7 ounces/ 210 g)

½ cup (125 ml) butter (1 stick)

2 cups (500 ml) confectioners' sugar

1 to 2 teaspoons milk

METHOD

1. Preheat oven to 350°F (177°C). Line muffin tins with paper or foil liners. Whisk together flour, graham cracker crumbs, baking powder, salt and cinnamon.

2. Using an electric mixer on medium-high speed, cream butter, brown sugar and honey until light and fluffy. Reduce speed to medium and beat in eggs and vanilla, scraping down the sides of the bowl as necessary. Add flour mixture, mix well.

3. Divide batter between lined muffin tins, filling each three-quarters full. Bake until cake tester inserted in centers comes out with only a few crumbs attached, about 25 minutes. Rotate tins halfway through the baking process, to promote even baking. Remove from oven, transfer tins to wire racks to cool for 10 minutes, turn out cupcakes onto racks and continue to cool.

For Chocolate Ganache Glaze:

1. Place finely chopped chocolate in a medium heatproof bowl. In a small saucepan, over medium-high heat bring cream and corn syrup to a simmer. Pour cream mixture over chocolate. Let stand, until chocolate begins to melt.

2. Using a flexible spatula, gently stir cream and chocolate until totally combined, or until mixture is glossy and smooth.

3. Spoon 2 teaspoons of glaze on top of each cooled cupcake.

For Marshmallow Frosting:

1. Remove and discard lid and foil seal from jar of marshmallow creme. Place jar in the microwave for 15 to 20 seconds to soften marshmallow creme. In a large bowl, beat marshmallow creme, butter and confectioners' sugar on low speed, until combined. Beat in milk, ½ teaspoon at a time, until the right consistency is reached.

2. Spoon or pipe frosting over glazed cupcakes. Serve.

Black Bottom Cupcakes with Cream Cheese

PREP TIME: 20 min
BAKING TIME: 20–25 min

---

makes 20 cupcakes

INGREDIENTS

8 ounces (240 g) cream cheese, room temperature

4 fresh eggs, divided

⅓ cup (75 ml) granulated sugar

2 cups (500 ml) unbleached all-purpose flour

1 cup (250 ml) brown sugar, packed

½ cup (125 ml) granulated sugar

¾ cup (175 ml) unsweetened cocoa powder

½ teaspoon baking soda

1 teaspoon baking powder

½ teaspoon salt

1 cup (250 ml) buttermilk

½ cup (125 ml) oil

2 teaspoons pure vanilla extract

METHOD

1. Preheat oven to 350°F (177°C). Line muffin tins with paper or foil liners.

2. In a small mixing bowl, beat cream cheese, 1 egg and ⅓ cup granulated sugar until light, smooth and creamy. Set aside.

3. In a large bowl, combine flour, brown sugar, ½ cup (125 ml) granulated sugar, cocoa powder, baking soda, baking powder and salt; mix well. In a separate bowl, beat buttermilk, remaining eggs, oil and vanilla until well combined. Add buttermilk mixture to flour mixture; beat for about 2 minutes, scraping the sides of the bowl as necessary.

4. Divide batter between lined muffin tins, filling them two-thirds full. Spoon a heaping tablespoon of the cream cheese mixture over each filled cup; gently swirl with the tip of a knife to get the marbled effect.

5. Bake until cake tester inserted in centers comes out clean, about 20 to 25 minutes. Rotate tins halfway through the baking process, to promote even baking. Remove from oven; cool in pan for 5 minutes. Remove cupcakes from pan and transfer to wire racks to cool completely.

Doodle Bug Cupcakes (Kid's Favorite)

PREP TIME: 30 min
BAKING TIME: 20 min

makes 24 cupcakes

INGREDIENTS

1 package white cake mix (without pudding in the mix)

1 cup (250 ml) sour cream

3 eggs

⅓ cup (75 ml) water

⅓ cup (75 ml) canola oil

1 teaspoon pure vanilla extract

1½ cups (350 ml) prepared cream cheese or vanilla frosting

Food coloring: blue, green, red, and yellow

Red or black licorice strings, cut into 2-inch (5 cm) pieces

Assorted round candies, such as M & M's or Skittles

METHOD

1. Preheat oven to 350°F (177°C). Line muffin tins with paper or foil liners.

2. In a large bowl, using an electric mixer set on low speed, beat cake mix, sour cream, eggs, water, oil and vanilla together for 1 minute, or until blended. Increase mixer speed to medium and beat for 1 or 2 minutes, or until batter is smooth.

3. Divide batter evenly between lined muffin tins, filling them two-thirds full. Bake until cake tester inserted in centers comes out clean, about 20 minutes. Rotate tins halfway through the baking process, to promote even baking. Remove from oven, cool cupcakes in the pans on wire racks for 5 minutes. Remove from pans and cool completely on wire racks before frosting.

4. Divide frosting between 4 bowls. Add food coloring, one drop at a time, to each bowl until desired color is achieved. Using an offset spatula, frost the tops of the cupcakes. Using a wooden toothpick, poke three holes on opposite sides of each cupcake, making six holes total. To make legs, insert licorice piece into each hole. Decorate cupcakes with assorted candies.

Sticky Date Pudding Cupcakes

PREP TIME: 35 min
BAKING TIME: 14–15 min

makes 12 cupcakes

INGREDIENTS

FOR CARAMEL-RUM SAUCE:

½ cup (125 ml) dark brown sugar

¼ cup (60 ml) heavy cream

4 tablespoons unsalted butter

1 tablespoon dark rum

FOR STICKY DATE PUDDING:

1¼ cups (300 ml) water

1 tablespoon pure vanilla extract

1 cup (250 ml) dates, coarsely chopped

½ teaspoon baking soda

1 cup plus 2 tablespoons (280 ml)
all-purpose flour

1¼ teaspoons baking powder

¼ teaspoon salt

4 tablespoons unsalted butter, room
temperature

½ cup plus 2 tablespoons (155 ml)
granulated sugar

2 large eggs

Sweetened whipped cream, for garnish

METHOD

For Caramel-Rum Sauce:

In a medium stainless steel saucepan, combine brown sugar, heavy cream, butter and rum. Cover over medium heat, whisking constantly, until smooth. Set aside and keep warm.

For Sticky Date Pudding:

1. Position oven rack in the center of the oven and preheat to 350°F (177°C). Generously grease standard size muffin tins and set aside.

2. In a small saucepan, bring the water, vanilla extract and chopped dates to a boil. Remove from heat and stir in the baking soda (the mixture will foam up). Cover the saucepan and set aside.

3. In a medium bowl, using a wire whisk, stir together the flour, baking powder and salt until thoroughly combined.

4. In a 4½ quart (4¼ liter) bowl of a heavy duty mixer, using the paddle attachment, beat the butter and sugar for 30 seconds at medium speed. Add the eggs one at a time, beating between each addition. Scrape down the sides of the bowl as needed with a rubber spatula.

5. At low speed beat in half of the flour mixture, mix in the dates with their liquid and then the remaining flour mixture. Divide the mixture evenly among the prepared muffin tins. Bake for 10 minutes, or until barely set. Remove the pan from the oven and spoon 1 tablespoon of the caramel-rum sauce over each one. Return pan to oven and bake for an additional 4 to 5 minutes. Remove from oven; set pan on a wire rack and allow to cool for 5 minutes.

6. Carefully unmold each pudding and place on a dessert plate. Serve with the remaining sauce and whipped cream.

Zucchini Cupcakes

PREP TIME: 20 min
BAKING TIME: 20 min

makes 24 cupcakes

INGREDIENTS

3 cups (750 ml) unbleached all-purpose flour

1/2 teaspoon baking powder

1 teaspoon baking soda

1 teaspoon salt

1/2 teaspoon nutmeg

2 teaspoons ground cinnamon

1/4 teaspoon cloves

1 cup (250 ml) vegetable oil

2 fresh large eggs

1 tablespoon vanilla extract

2 cups (500 ml) light-brown sugar, packed

3 cups (750 ml) grated zucchini, packed

1 cup (250 ml) walnuts, coarsely chopped (optional)

Confectioners' sugar, for dusting

METHOD

1. Preheat oven to 350°F (177°C). Line muffin tins with paper or foil liners. In a large bowl, whisk together the first seven ingredients. In a separate large bowl, whisk together oil, eggs and vanilla and mix well. Whisk in brown sugar and mix until smooth. Add zucchini, stirring to incorporate; add flour mixture and stir until just combined. Stir in walnuts, if using.

2. Divide batter evenly between lined tins, filling each one three-quarters full. Bake for 20 minutes or until a cake tester inserted in the middle comes out clean. Rotate tins halfway through the baking process to promote even baking.

3. Transfer tins to a wire rack; let cool completely before turning out cupcakes. Dust with confectioners' sugar. Serve.

Pistachio Cupcakes

PREP TIME: 15 min
BAKING TIME: 18-22 min

makes 24 cupcakes

INGREDIENTS

1 package yellow cake mix

1 package pistachio pudding

3 eggs

¾ cup (175 ml) oil

1 cup (250 ml) 7-Up or water

1 teaspoon pure vanilla extract

FOR FROSTING:

1 package pistachio pudding mix

1½ cups (350 ml) milk

9 ounces (270 g) whipped topping, thawed

METHOD

1. Preheat oven to 350°F (177°C). Line muffin tins with paper or foil cupcake liners. In a large bowl, mix cake mix and pudding together. Add the eggs and oil, mix well. Add the 7-Up or water and vanilla; mix until just blended.

2. Divide batter evenly between the prepared tins, filling each two-thirds full. Bake for 18 to 22 minutes or until cupcakes are slightly brown and a cake tester inserted in the center comes out clean. Remove from oven, cool in pans on wire racks for about 5 minutes. Remove cupcakes from tins and cool completely before frosting.

For Frosting:

Mix pudding mix and milk together until thick and creamy. Add whipped topping mixing until well blended. Frost cooled cupcakes using an offset spatula. Refrigerate cupcakes until ready to serve.

■ TIP

Frosted cupcakes must be refrigerated.

Angel Food Cupcakes with Strawberry Topping

PREP TIME: 20 min

BAKING TIME: 15–18 min

---

makes 18 cupcakes

INGREDIENTS

½ cup (125 ml) cake flour

⅔ cup (150 ml) confectioners' sugar

6 large egg whites

1 pinch salt

¾ teaspoon cream of tartar

½ cup (125 ml) granulated sugar

2 teaspoons pure almond extract

FOR FROSTING:

1 package (3.4 ounces/102 g) Strawberry or Raspberry JELL-O

1 cup (250 ml) boiling water

1 package frozen strawberries or raspberries

1 pint (½ L) whipping cream

METHOD

1. Preheat oven to 350°F (177°C). Line muffin tins with paper or foil liners. Sift flour and confectioners' sugar together several times; set aside.

2. In a large bowl, beat egg whites and salt together until frothy. Add the cream of tartar, continue beating until soft peaks form. Gradually add granulated sugar, beating until stiff peaks form. Using a rubber spatula, fold in the flour and confectioners' sugar mixture one-third at a time. Fold in the almond extract.

3. Divide batter between prepared muffin tins, filling them three-quarters full. Bake until lightly browned on top or about 15 to 18 minutes. Rotate tins halfway through the baking process to promote even baking. Remove from oven, cool for 5 minutes in tins on wire racks. Remove cupcakes from tins and cool completely on wire racks before frosting.

For Frosting:

Mix JELL-O and boiling water, stirring until dissolved. Add frozen fruit. Chill until set. Beat the whipping cream until soft peaks form. Add JELL-O mixture slowly. Frost cupcakes. Keep refrigerated until ready to serve.

Easy Cookies and Cream Cheesecake Cupcakes

PREP TIME: 20 min
BAKING TIME: 22 min
CHILLING TIME: 4 h

makes 30 cupcakes

INGREDIENTS

42 chocolate cream-filled sandwich cookies, such as Oreos (30 left whole and 12 coarsely chopped)

2 pounds (900 g) softened cream cheese (4 8-ounce packages)

1 cup (250 ml) granulated sugar

1 teaspoon pure vanilla extract

4 fresh large eggs, lightly beaten

1 cup (250 ml) sour cream

¼ teaspoon kosher salt

FOR BUTTERCREAM FROSTING:

1½ cups (450 ml) unsalted butter, softened (3 sticks)

3¾ cups (900 ml) confectioners' sugar, sifted

1 teaspoon pure vanilla extract

METHOD

1. Preheat oven to 275°F (135°C). Line muffin tins with paper or foil liners and place one whole cookie in each lined muffin tin.

2. In a large bowl, using an electric mixer on medium-high speed, beat cream cheese until smooth and creamy. Scrape down the sides of the bowl as necessary. Gradually add sugar and vanilla, beat until combined. Slowly pour in eggs, beating to blend, scraping down the sides of the bowl as needed. Beat in sour cream and salt. Stir in chopped cookies by hand.

3. Evenly divide batter between cookie-filled muffin tins, filling each one almost to the top. Bake for about 22 minutes or until filling has set. Rotate tins halfway through the baking process to promote even baking. Transfer tins to wire racks to cool completely. Refrigerate in the tins for at least 4 hours or overnight. Remove cupcakes from tins just prior to serving.

For Buttercream Frosting:

1. In a medium bowl, using an electric mixer on medium-high speed, beat butter for about two minutes, or until light and creamy.

2. Reduce mixer speed to medium. Add confectioners' sugar ½ cup (125 ml) at a time, beating after each addition. Add vanilla, and beat until buttercream is smooth.

3. Spread frosting on cupcakes using a small offset spatula. Serve.

Raspberry Cream Cupcakes

PREP TIME: 20 min
BAKING TIME: 18–22 min

makes 30 cupcakes

INGREDIENTS

2¾ cups (650 ml) unbleached all-purpose flour

2½ teaspoons baking powder

½ teaspoon kosher salt

1¾ cups (400 ml) granulated sugar

¾ cup (175 ml) unsalted butter, room temperature (1½ sticks)

1 teaspoon pure vanilla extract

1 teaspoon almond extract

4 fresh large eggs

2 egg yolks

1½ cups (350 ml) milk

FOR RASPBERRY CREAM FILLING:

1 cup (250 ml) heavy whipping cream, chilled

¼ cup (60 ml) confectioners' sugar

1 teaspoon pure vanilla extract

1 pint (½ L) fresh raspberries, rinsed and patted dry

METHOD

1. Preheat oven to 350°F (177°C). Line muffin tins with paper or foil liners.

2. In a medium bowl, combine flour, baking powder, and salt. In a separate bowl, using an electric mixer set on medium speed, beat sugar, butter, vanilla and almond extract until light and fluffy, about 4 minutes. One at a time, add eggs and egg yolks, beating well after each addition. Add flour mixture and milk, alternating between the two. Beat well after each addition, scrape the sides of the bowl as needed.

3. Divide batter between lined muffin tins, filling them three-quarters full. Bake until cake tester inserted in centers comes out clean, about 18 to 22 minutes. Rotate tins halfway through the baking process to promote even baking. Remove from oven, cool cupcakes in the tins on wire racks for 15 minutes. Remove cupcakes from tins and let cool completely on wire racks before filling.

For Raspberry Cream Filling:

1. In a large bowl, using an electric mixer at high speed, beat chilled whipping cream and confectioners' sugar together until stiff peaks form, about 5 minutes. Add vanilla and beat for another minute.

2. Place raspberries in a small bowl and mash lightly with a fork. Gently fold raspberries into whipped cream until well blended.

To Assemble:

Gently cut tops from each cupcake; spread with raspberry cream filling. Replace cupcake tops and sprinkle with confectioners' sugar. Serve.